STROUD AS IT WAS

Joan Tucker

This book is dedicated to all Stroud exiles, those who were born here and those who were not.

Stroud from Rodborough Hill in the 1860's from a print published by J. Elliott, Bookseller, High Street, Stroud.

Published by Hendon Publishing Co., Ltd., Hendon Mill, Nelson, Lancs.
Text © F. J. Tucker, 1978.
Printed by Turner & Earnshaw Ltd., Westway House, Sycamore Avenue, Burnley, Lancs.

Foreword

Stroud is in the Cotswolds, but
although it is surrounded by what
has been officially designated as
'an area of outstanding natural
beauty', it is specifically excluded
from that designation. Stroud is,
and always has been, a workaday
place. It has never been recomm-
ended by guidebooks, and has been
thought to hold little interest for
photographers. My task in compiling
this book of old photographs has
therefore not been easy, and as I
particularly wanted to show as
many facets of Stroud life as possible,
it has been necessary for me to ask
the help of a large number of
people. That help has been given
willingly and most generously, and
to each and every one I owe a debt
of gratitude. I regret that the scope
of the book has been limited to the
vicinity of Stroud itself, but perhaps
in the future it will be possible to
add another volume to encompass
the valleys as a whole.

1. The Church as it faces the Shambles, showing the south aisle and porch believed to have been built at the end of C15th by the Whittington family of Lypiatt, (Stroud claims to be the home of Dick Whittington). A vestry room was built over the porch in 1806 and the arms of the Whittington family re-erected over the doorway. The sundial was placed over the vestry window on 5th March 1832, the same year that 113 children were baptised on Whit Sunday between noon and 5.00 p.m.

The new chancel can be seen here. It cost the Churchwardens £250 to build it in 1787.

Fortunately, this and the photographs overleaf were taken in 1866 just before the old Parish Church was pulled down and the present Church built on the old foundations. Only the fourteenth century tower and some of the old monuments still remain.

Originally Stroud was part of the parish of Bisley, and a little Chapel-of-Ease was built here to serve the inhabitants of this far-flung hamlet. When the larger church was built in the C.14th, the chapel became the Chancel. Gradually over the next 500 years alterations were made to the fabric until it had changed character completely from Gothic to C.18th utilitarian.

2. *Above:* The nave and chancel. The hexagonal oak pulpit originally had an ornate sounding board suspended from the ceiling by an iron rod. The large round-headed east window was specially made for the convenience of Rev. Wm. Ellis who was the near-sighted Curate-in-Charge when alterations were made in the late C18th. When the organ was installed in the gallery over the tower arch, windows were put in the roof to give extra light and ventilation. Lighting was by candles until 10th March 1839, thereafter by gas.

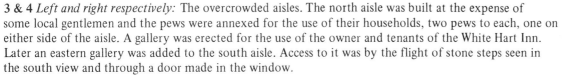

3 & 4 *Left and right respectively:* The overcrowded aisles. The north aisle was built at the expense of some local gentlemen and the pews were annexed for the use of their households, two pews to each, one on either side of the aisle. A gallery was erected for the use of the owner and tenants of the White Hart Inn. Later an eastern gallery was added to the south aisle. Access to it was by the flight of stone steps seen in the south view and through a door made in the window.

5. *Right:* The top of the High Street at the beginning of this century. The two large matching C18th buildings are mentioned in Fisher's Notes and Recollections' as being divided into two and three houses with shops in each. The lowest shop was once occupied by Mr. Nayler, an apothecary, who died in 1780. One of his sons rose to become Sir George Nayler, Knight, Garter Principal King at Arms and F.S.A.

Later the house was the business premises of a tailor, Joshua Holder, who had as one of his journeymen Benjamin Parsons, later to become the Minister of Ebley Chapel under the Countess of Huntingdon's Connexion.

Both of these buildings have been demolished, but the two old Cotswold houses in between them remain. At the time of this photograph the lower one was The Nelson Inn, and the next one was a gin parlour connected with it. Its early C19th shop front, now Mrs Barsby's sweet shop can be seen clearly.

The Cross: Originally the centre of the town where the roads to Bisley and to Chalford met, and for many years the site of the Friday market and the two annual fairs held in May and August. The butchers and butter women had their stalls at the Shambles but corn was sold at the Cross and the pig pens were there until the cattle market was moved to Lansdown in 1889. The supply of water to Stroud was difficult until in 1769 Benjamin Glazebrook paid for water to be brought in lead pipes 2″ in diameter from Gainey's Well to a small round reservoir near the Cross. (This was still to be seen until about 1967 when the area was cleared for building the new Police Station). The public supply at the Cross remained unsatisfactory and after various attempts to deepen the well, and provide better machinery, the pump was removed to Paganhill in 1865 and replaced by a drinking fountain.

6. *Above::* An early photograph looking down the High Street showing signs of the photographers' usual difficulties. Some processes required an exposure of up to ten minutes, by which time half the subjects could have disappeared, leaving a ghost-like trace of themselves. Note the donkey shape on the left of the fountain.

7. *Right:* Facing up Nelson Street about the turn of the century. The delivery basket probably belonged to a carrier who was in business nearby. Mark Merrett was the photographer.

8. The occasion is the 'Stroud News' annual outing to London. The date is about 1900, or just before the flat-roofed extension was built on to the main buildings of the G.W.R. station. Each year the Stroud News hired a special train to take staff and friends to London, and any extra tickets were sold to the public. The last excursion took place in 1924 when a visit was made to the British Empire Exhibition at Wembley, described in the official guide as a 'Family Party of the British Empire'.

9. *Left:* The corner of High Street and King Street just before the road widening and rebuilding in 1904; hence the clearance sale being advertised on the windows of C.B. Gardner's shop. The idea was to level off the street to align it with the entrance to Lansdown. A policeman stood on point duty here for many years.

The tricorne hat seen on the corner of the building bore the inscription 'Established 1805'. It was replaced after the rebuilding, and remained until 1964, when the business closed, thus marking nearly 160 years of a family business of hatters and hosiers in Stroud. In the beginning all the hats sold were made on the premises. Later the firm specialised in the dressing and restoring of silk hats, which were the standard headgear for business and professional gentlemen. When Mr. A. Gardner retired he reminisced "At the time when everyone wore bowlers, they sold for 2/6d. or 3/-d., but if you paid 5/6d. you had a tip-top fur hat with a silk lining".

10. *Left:* Trade-card of William Sims (c. 1851). William Thomas Sims started his business in High Street in 1850, and soon became an important figure in the town. He was a member of the local Board of Health and Stroud Urban District Council, being its Chairman for many years. The High Street shop was leased to Thos. Lipton's in 1900. When Sims died in 1917, he left £1,000 for erecting a clock in Stroud (Sims clock . . . completed February 1921) and £2,000 for entertaining the poor of Stroud and Uplands to a Christmas dinner. This is now part of the Stroud United Charities.

11. Town Time and the view along King Street about 1910. This corner derives its name from the clock in the wall on the right of the picture. It was used as the trade mark of Robert Bragg, "Jeweller, Optician and Watchmaker", who was in business at Number 1, High Street in 1867. In an advertisement in Morris's Directory he states that it 'may always be relied on as the standard of exact Greenwich or Railway time and now fitted with an Automatic Illuminating Apparatus, it is available for public use both night and day'. Actually it is a watchmaker's regulator, and as such is usually kept inside his premises, and not outside.

Further along on the right is the Green Dragon. Its distinctive facade is not often clearly seen in photographs. The licensee standing outside is probably Charles Pocket. It was a tied house of Godsells Brewery. Fortunatley when new owners made it into a supermarket in 1959, they planned for the upper storeys to be propped up on stilts while the shop and warehouse were built below, thus very little change to the atmosphere of the street was effected at that time.

12. *Top left:* The Police Station Badbrook. 21st June 1907. The celebrations were for the fourth visit of the Gloucestershire Agricultural Society to Stroud for their annual show. The honour was duly appreciated by the townsfolk, and the whole town was 'en fete'. The Midland Railway laid on special excursions, and 'Welcome to Stroud' streamers were hung around. Floral decorated arches were erected in High St., George St., and Gloucester St., and an agricultural arch in King St. A competition was held for the best illuminated premises and this was won by the Imperial Hotel (using gas lights and Japanese lanterns) with the Police Station coming second.

The show itself was held in a field in Stratford Park. There was a 300 foot grandstand, seating 1500 people, a bandstand, roped enclosure for riding and driving, sheep and cattle pens etc., but no pigs, by order, because of an outbreak of swine fever.

13. *Bottom left:* The Millinery Show Room of Sidney B. Park's Draper's shop in 1903. The shop was at the corner of King Street and George Street, on the site now occupied by the Midland Bank. The Park family at one time lived in a flat over the shop, and several members of Alice Bingle's family were in service there. She has written a little about it in her book 'Life in an English Valley', published in U.S.A.

The firm spent a lot of time and trouble decorating their premises for various events, like Jubilees, and agricultural shows, and won prizes for it. Mr. Park gave Park Gardens in Slad Road to the town in memory of his only son Herbert who was killed in France in 1917, aged twenty three.

14. *Right:* Old Agricultural Arch erected between the Royal George Hotel and Coleys, the chemist in King Street in 1912, for the Agricultural and Horticultural Show. It is probably the same as the one previously put up in 1907. Then it was described in the 'Stroud Journal' as painted in an old-fashioned style in grey water colour on canvas and depicting farming scenes.

The work was done by George Freebury of the firm of Philip Ford and Son. This well known local firm with premises in Slad Road carried on business as builders and decorators, wheelwrights and undertakers. In a trade advertisement of 1904, they describe the carts and vans which they make specially strong 'with a view to the trying nature of the local roads'.

15. *Top left:* The Royal George Hotel can be seen from the top of George Street in this view taken about 1910. The projecting clock over the premises of Alfred Burton, jeweller, optician and silversmith was removed in 1911 and replaced by . . . . . . 'a pair of specs, A useful item in a general way, But not much good to tell the time o' day.'

Thus wrote 'J.W.' to the Stroud News. The clock was back in its place soon afterwards, but the specs remained underneath it. Plans to light this street (then known as Great George Street) were made in 1833 by the Stroud Gas Co., and one of the original holders can be seen on the Bedford Street corner.

16. *Bottom left:* A Diamond Jubilee (1897) procession coming up Russell Street. The bowler-hatted gentleman driving a trap in the foreground is Mr. Henry Thomas Pearce, blacksmith, of London Road, and the boy is probably one of his apprentices.

In the background workmen are building the Wilts. and Dorset Bank (now the National Westminster). It was due to be opened in the following year, when the bank was going to move from its premises in the High Street into the new building.

17. *Top left:* Subscription Rooms. Ever since they were built by public subscription in 1833, the rooms have been the principle meeting place for social and political gatherings. A dinner was given in honour of Lord John Russell when he was elected to the Borough. Balls, charity bazaars, and concerts were held here, and Poole's Myromama aroused great interest when it came in the eighteen-nineties.

The porte-cochere was added in 1869 and a one-way system for carriages was arranged, as seen in the picture. The cannons were from Sebastopol.

18. *Bottom left:* London Road about the time of the Great War. The sign of the white horse on the left marks the premises of Mr. Pearce's blacksmith's and farrier's shop (see No.16). Further along where the people are standing is the Empire Theatre with many gas lamps overhanging the pavement.

Opposite was Isaac Lendon's Coachbuilding works, and then, nearer to the camera is the row of shops which still exist today, although the roofline has altered. Messrs. Baker Bros. has now crossed over the road.

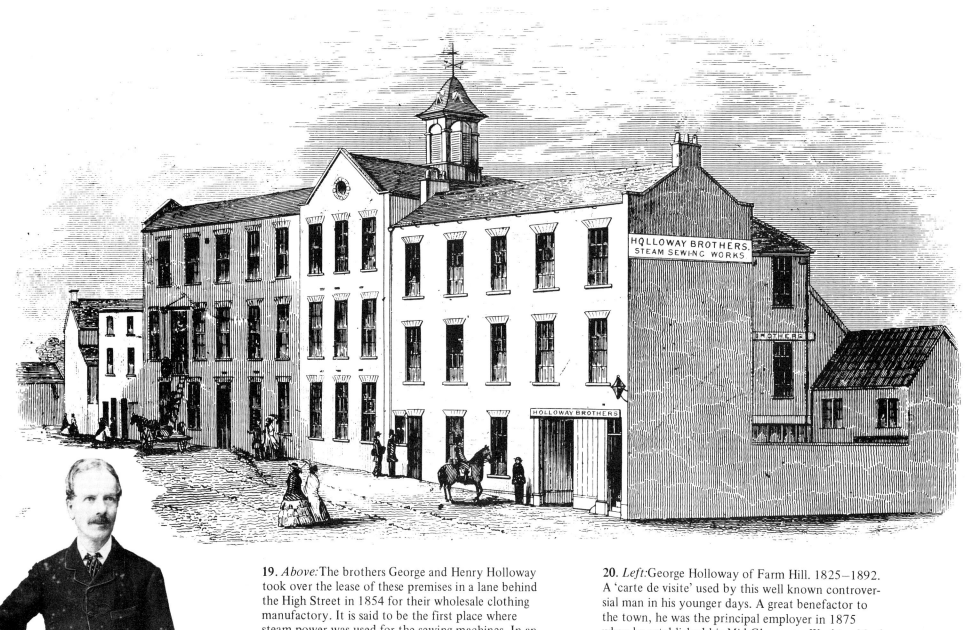

19. *Above:* The brothers George and Henry Holloway took over the lease of these premises in a lane behind the High Street in 1854 for their wholesale clothing manufactory. It is said to be the first place where steam power was used for the sewing machines. In an advertisement dated 13th May, in the Stroud Journal, of that year the firm states 'We are at present building a place large enough to produce 2,000 pairs of trousers per week . . . the whole of the machines to work by steam power'. Consequently the lane became known as Threadneedle Street.

20. *Left:* George Holloway of Farm Hill. 1825–1892. A 'carte de visite' used by this well known controversial man in his younger days. A great benefactor to the town, he was the principal employer in 1875 when he established his Mid-Gloucester Working Men's Conservative Association Benefit Society. The motto was 'God helps those who help themselves'. He was M.P. for the Stroud Division from 1886 until his death.

21. *Top right:* Stroud Sanitary Laundry Co. Ltd., occupied premises with a drying ground near Ebley mills leased from Sir Wm. H. Marling in 1891. A lot of women were employed in a big light airy room with a double bank of windows down each side and at the end; not the usual sort of conditions associated with laundry work. In fact, in later views of the interior which I have seen, it appears that curtains were put up at the windows. Possibly there was too much light.

No Work of an Undesirable Kind Received.

22. *Bottom right:* Ebley Brass Band in 1910. Stroud people have always been proud of their brass bands and often several members of one family would belong to one. Here Mr. Stephen Hook of Cainscross is the seventeen year old cornet player in the middle of the back row.

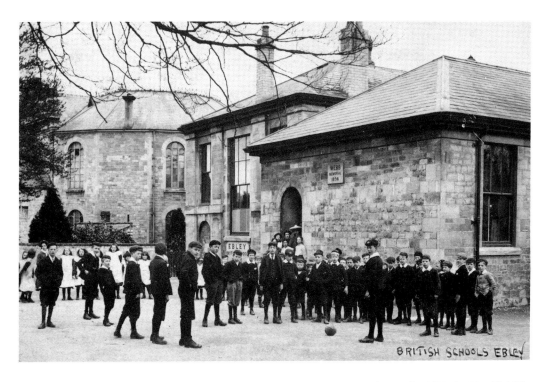

BRITISH SCHOOLS EBLEY

23. *Top left:* The British Schools, Ebley. The Rev. Benjamin Parsons was appointed Minister of Ebley Chapel under the Countess of Huntingdon's Trust in 1826 at the age of twenty nine. He remained in Ebley until the end of his life in 1855, devoting himself to the needs of the workers in the village community. Being a self-educated man himself, he was responsible for creating a thirst for education in others, and his evening classes in Botany and animal life were especially well attended. By 1840 the people had raised enough money themselves to build a school, and so successful was it that the master would often be woken at 5.00 a.m. by men and women who wanted to have lessons before they started their daily work. Rev. Parson's book 'Education the Birthright of every Human Being' was published in 1845. The first headmaster was Henry Webb, a man who had every sympathy with the workers' lot. He was also one of the founders of the Cainscross and Ebley Co-operative Society, formed in 1863. When the school was altered in 1896, two more classrooms were added as a memorial to his forty years at Ebley, as 'a prince among teachers'. Originally there had been a main building with an upstairs and a small wing for infants.

24. *Bottom left:* Cainscross Brewery about 1904. Owned then by Carpenter & Co., Ale and Stout brewers who were renowned for the way they looked after their employees so well, crediting them with a bonus each year. The barley was malted on the premises and special attention was given to cleanliness throughout the processes. It was said that a fine beer was produced, and there were no tied houses, according to the trade description in the 'Pictorial Record for Stroud and District' published at that time.

25. *Right:* Strachan & Co. Ltd. the firm who have occupied both Lodgemore and Fromehall mills since 1866 carried on the tradition of the Stroud valleys by producing superfine broad cloths. They supplied (and still do) scarlet and blue cloth for the officers of the army and navy, billiard-table cloth, hunting and livery clothes of every shade, in addition to the more sombre woollen cloth required for everyday wear. They won the highest awards at all the big international exhibitions which they attended. All these photographs were taken in 1937, but the processes in woollen manufacture have hardly changed over the years.

Spinning, Lodgemore.

Carding department, Fromehall.

Weaving, Lodgemore.

Setting teazles, Fromehall. At one time grown locally, these are now imported from France.

26. *Left:* The Playne family at Longfords House on the occasion of the Coming of Age of the eldest son, W.H. Playne on 24th October, 1891. He is seated in the middle of the back row, with his father, Arthur Twisden Playne, the Author of 'A History of Minchinhampton and Avening' on his left. His mother, Mary is second from the left on the front row. She was one of the daughters of Richard Potter of Standish House, Chairman of the G.W.R. Her sister Theresa was the wife of C.A. Cripps (Lord Parmoor) and they stayed at Longfords in 1893, when he was adopted Conservative candidate for the Stroud Division. She died suddenly of a throat infection shortly afterwards. The Playnes are notable among the families of clothiers who owned water mills in the eighteenth century, and through hard work and enterprise continued to prosper through many generations. On this festive day a huge dinner tent was erected in the grounds above the mill, and photographs were also taken of the servants (see plate 31) and of the smaller presents . . . . books, briefcase, etc.

27. *Top right:* The Paganhill Maypole. There has been a maypole at Paganhill almost continuously since time immemorial. Each Whitsuntide the inhabitants would embellish it. At times it would be taken down and laid on the ground outside the wall of Field Place for repainting. Usually the re-erection ceremony took place on a Saturday afternoon, and all the village turned out to watch. These photographs show two such occasions. They were lent to me by Mr. J. Blick, who is a native of Paganhill. His father is the man in the straw hat on the near side of the maypole in the top picture, taken in 1911. The cottage with the shop window has now been demolished for road widening. Otherwise there had been very little change when the new maypole was erected in 1977 to mark the Silver Jubilee.

28. *Bottom right:* Mr. Blick's father is helping again at the ceremony in the late 1920's, along with, on his left, Mr. Barrett smoking a pipe. The man behind him, smoking a cigarette, in the centre of the picture, is Mr. Cordy, while with his back to the camera is Mr. Powell, gardener to the Stanton family at Field Place. Also with his hand on the rope is Mr. Joby Bayliss, who kept the old Crown Inn round the corner.

When Miss Stella Isacke was born in June 1877, her aunts, the Misses Isacke, had already earned a remarkable reputation for their Ladies College, first at Bellevue House, and then at Stratford Abbey. In Morris's Directory of 1876, it was advertised as having 'all the comforts of a Christian home . . . with the privileges and refinements of a family. Healthful moral training, high mental culture, with self-government and habits of industry are the chief points aimed at.'

The curriculum seems to be more enlightened than is usual for the time, because in addition to the attainments a young lady was normally expected to have, like music, singing, drawing, dancing and calisthenics; science, including biology and chemistry and mathematics were also included, as well as French, German, and Latin. In all this the principals were assisted by eight masters and five resident governesses (the latter took the pupils for daily walks as one of their duties). Later Miss Stella, who lived to be 100 years old, took over the running of the school with her two sisters, at a time when the girls were the envy of other school-girls in the town because of their smart uniform. Dark blue skirt with white shirt and blue and brown striped tie, plus a Saxe-blue blazer jacket with cloche hat to match and brown shoes and stockings was the regulation outfit.

29. *Top right:* Stratford Abbey College. The front with rose walk and garden wall facing Stratford Road. Now the site of Townsend's car park.

30. *Bottom right:* The entrance hall with delicate openwork staircase. The private post box was made specially for the school, and is today one of the proud possessions of a former neighbour.

31. *Far right:* The servants of the Playne family at Longfords house in 1891. I regret that they are all anonymous now as no note had been made of their names in the family album. (see also plate 26).

32. *Top left:* Stroud Volunteer Fire Brigade, taken outside the Old Vicarage in Lansdown in July 1909. Kelly's Directory of 1902 records that the Brigade had a captain and eleven men, a steam fire engine, a fire escape which extended to 45 feet and other appliances. The captain, Mr. Philip Ford, had taken over in 1893, and remained in charge for 38 years. His son, Mr. Frank Ford, was his 2nd officer. First established in 1868 to supplement the official town brigade, the Volunteers were supported by public subscription, and concerts were held on their behalf. They represented Stroud at the Review of Fire Brigades held by Queen Victoria at Windsor in 1887.

33. *Bottom left:* Fire at Stratford Mill. The mills in the Stroud valleys are prone to severe fires because the oil used in the manufacture of cloth seeped into the wooden floors. The oil, variously rape oil, olive oil, or even butter or animal grease, was added to the wool after dyeing, before scribbling and carding, to make it easier to handle. Stratford Mill had been bought by R. Townsend & Son, in 1901, for the manufacture of cattle cake, and their corn seed and farm fertilizer business.

34. *Top right:* The same engine decorated in honour of the Coronation of King George Vth. June 1911. The photograph was taken in the Shambles, where the fire engines were kept. The horses were stabled at Badbrook and when an alarm was given there would be a wild charge up Gloucester Street.

35. *Bottom right:* The new motor fire engine being christened in King Street Parade in 1919. Afterwards a display was given at the Wallbridge Canal basin. The Stroud Picture House (formerly the George Tap) is in the background.

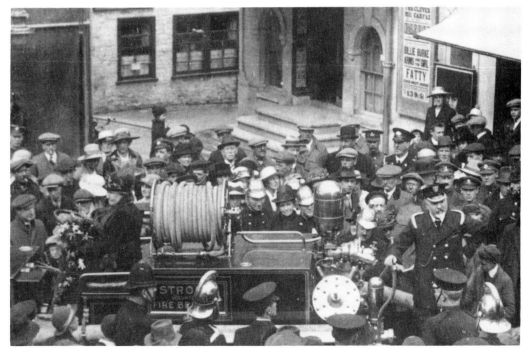

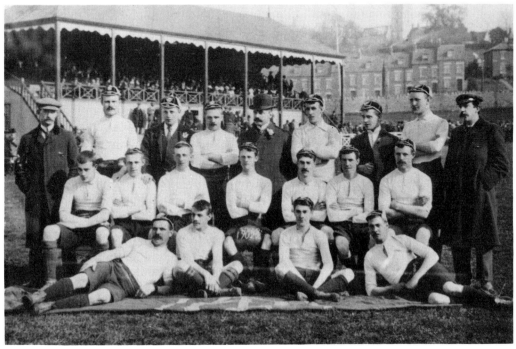

36. *Top left:* The Ritz Cinema when first opened in 1939. Shortly afterwards it was being used as one of the British Restaurants. A severe fire caused its closure in June 1961. Situated behind King Street Parade, it was close to where one of the town's earlier picture houses had been, next to the Royal George Hotel.

37. *Bottom left:* Stroud Rugby Club. The renowned team of the record 1902/3 season when 33 matches were played, of which 21 were won, 11 lost, and one was drawn. The team is, from left to right: J.T. Curtis, (Match Secretary), F.W. Harrison, G. Matthews, J. Whiley, D.R. Crosby (President) G. Fowkes, A. Brown, J. Mathews, F. Wheatley, (Hon Secretary). H. Chew, (Vice Captain), W.J. Kibblewhite, Lewis Smith, B. Blanch (Captain), T.W. Cull, S. Blanch, W. Partridge. W. Shewell, F. Brown, W.S. Cull, H. Smith.

These names represent several families which have been associated with rugby in Stroud for many years . . . the Blanchs, Culls, Smiths, and Wheatleys, while Shewell became the trainer in the 1920s.

Founded in the early 1870's, Stroud Rugby Club first played near Stratford Court but after a sad occasion when a player collapsed during a match, and died soon afterwards, they were asked to find another venue. Matches were played at Farmhill until the move to Fromehall Park in 1884-85 season.

The attractive pavilion was built about 1896 for £400, but was destroyed by fire in 1919. For many years the players had to change at Wallbridge, first in the Ship Inn, and then the Bell Hotel, and run half a mile to the ground.

38. *Right:* Stroud Cricket Club. The team of 1898, comprising, left to right: A.J. Hooper, (scorer), H. Poole, F. Whiting (professional), L.J. Lane W.J.W. Wilson (umpire), R.T. Godsell, J.J. Stephens and W.F.B. Warman (captains), W.A. Smith, D. Chambers, E.L. Warman, C. Merrett, J.E. Jefferies, and M.T. Wollright.

The club was started, it is said, by a group of five friends who met in a Stroud pub in 1850, and continues to flourish. The great W.G. Grace came to Stroud on a few occasions, and played at the attractive ground at Farm Hill. In 1882 he was a member of the United England XI against the twenty-two of Stroud. In the first innings he was clean-bowled first ball. (He was just recovering from mumps at the time). In the second innings he made 43, but also happened to take twenty-three of the Stroud wickets in their two innings.

The elegant wooden pavilion with the unusual concave roof in the background was erected in the eighteen-nineties, and remains almost unaltered today.

39. *Four plates:* Stroud can claim a part in the history of English drama, for it was at the Parish Church on 17th July, 1808 that the great actor Edmund Kean married Miss Mary Chambres (sic), an actress nine years his senior. They had been among the company of travelling players who performed in some workshops in Bedford Street. Previously some buildings in Church Street had been used as a theatre by the Bath Theatre Company and about the year 1779 Mrs Siddons was there with them.

Now Stroud is the home of the Cotswold Players, a long-established and much respected amateur theatre company. It was the brain-child of novelist Constance Smedley, and her husband, artist Maxwell Armfield, and began in October 1911 after the huge success of the Pageant (shown here) which they had helped to organise.

The year 1911 had a record summer, and great crowds turned up at Fromehall Park when the Stroud Liberal Party held their 'Mid-Gloucestershire Historical Pageant of Progress' on September 2nd, 7th, and 9th. The words were written by Frank Gwynne Evans of Woodchester, whose Prologue ran thus:

> *'Tis our intent to set before your eyes*
> *From ancient record and from local tales*
> *The story of our Cotswold hills and vales,*
> *And from our living pictures you shall see*
> *The march of progress and of liberty.'*

There followed a series of nine episodes each illustrating major events in the history of the area, and each performed by different districts. It ended with 'Present day progress' described as ' a representation of the arts and industries flourishing today', followed by an Epilogue. Over 1000 performers took part, among them the late Daisy Cull (Mrs Parratt), who was one of the principal actresses with the Cotswold Players for the rest of her life.

Top far left: The Roman soldiers in the first episode organised by Mr. Charles Hill of Stonehouse.

Bottom far left: Lady Gytha on a litter. She gave refuge to the nuns of Berkeley c. AD. 1050. The performers in this episode came from Minchinhampton, Amberley, Woodchester and Avening.

Top left: Episode 9. Showing the float depicting 'Prosperity' and a representation of farming in the area.

Bottom left: A section of the crowd, which includes the present Mrs F.T. Hammond of Chalford and her sister.

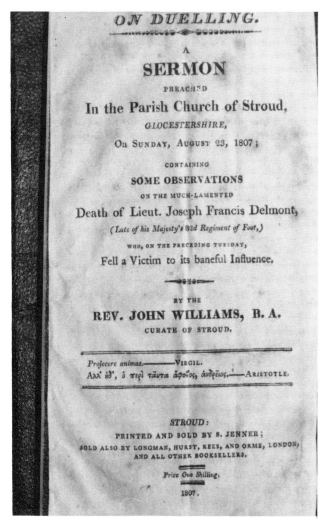

40. Title page of the sermon preached a few days after the fatal duel had taken place in Grange Fields between Lt. Delmont and Lt. Heazle, both recruiting officers for the war against Napoleon. Lt. Delmont is buried in the south-west corner of the churchyard. He was twenty one years old.

41. Rev. Dr. John Badcock, 1808–1885. Vicar of Stroud from 1865 until his death, Dr. Badcock was incumbent at a very difficult time. He arrived just after the decision to demolish the old church and build a new one had been made, and he was able to unite the parishioners in favour of it.

He took an interest in the Black Boy school, and visited to examine the pupils in reading, writing, and arithmetic, or to give a talk on the merits of punctuality. But more often his visit was for the purpose of giving the children a scramble of nuts and sweets.

42. A reproduction of an old postcard showing the spire being repaired after being struck by lightning in March 1878. Mr. W. Cheriton, a member of the choir is standing on one leg on the highest point. He was not the first one to perform such a feat. When a new weathercock was set up in 1828, one Henry Ayres stood on the finial to play 'God save the King' on his bugle.

43. *Top right:* Bank House at the corner of Lansdown and High Street, a snapshot taken early this century. It was built in brick in the eighteenth century supposedly by a baker named Alderley as it was for a long time known as 'Alderley's oven'. Fisher tells the story in his 'Notes and Recollections'.

For many years it was the premises of the Capital and Counties Bank and was ultimately sold to the Urban District Council for use as offices.

44. *Bottom right:* A snapshot taken in the private gardens behind Bank House at the bottom of High Street, possibly in the early nineteen-hundreds. On 8th July, 1930 Ernest Winterbotham and his two brothers presented the gardens to the town 'to be maintained in perpetuity in memory of their Father and Mother, Mr. & Mrs. Edward Winterbotham, who for many years enjoyed them as their private gardens'. The tall chimney seen behind the house is that of the Stroud Brewery Co. Ltd. in Rowcroft, and was erected in 1901.

BANK GARDENS STROUD.

45. *Left:* Bank Gardens. Some of the grateful townsfolk enjoying the peace and quiet of the avenue soon after the gardens were presented to the town.

46. *Right:* Merrywalks, Beeches Green and Badbrook. This view was taken from the railway viaduct by the firm of Frith and Co. about 1900. In the foreground are the long gardens behind the Rowcroft houses, stretching down to Slad brook. Beyond them is the Badbrook Mill and Old Armoury, where the multi-storey car park and bus station are now. Stroud Urban Council had begun to think about vehicle parking as early as 1914, when they purchased some stables and dressing boxes in Merrywalks for £1,500. Space for parking eight charabancs was later provided there. Badbrook House is behind the distant trees. It was demolished in the early 1960s to improve road visibility. The Roman Catholic Church at Beeches Green was built in 1858, and the Convent of St. Rose of Lima, next to it, in 1867. The road beneath them, now widened, bears the unusual name of Merrywalks, and gives much speculation as to its origin. It runs alongside the Slad brook which was the parish boundary. It could signify a boundary walk, the next parish being Painswick, dedicated to St. Mary - St. Mary's Walk?

47. *Top left:* The Grove, Chalford. Passengers seem to prefer the motor bus, rather than the horse brake waiting behind, to get them into Stroud. The same type of bus was also used on the Stroud-Painswick route earlier this century.

The G.W.R. began their service from Stroud station to Chalford in 1905, and it was merged into the Western National timetable in 1929.

48. *Bottom Left:* The Steam Launch 'IBEX' on the Thames and Severn Canal en route for Bristol having been built by the firm of Isaac J. Abdela and Mitchell Ltd. of the Hope Mills, Brimscombe. Mr. Abdela of Manchester, who is standing by the boiler in the photograph, had taken over the firm of Edwin Clark & Co. Ltd. in about 1898, and specialised in building stern wheel steamers built in sections for export to many parts of the world. The previous firm had built some of the steamers which ply the Thames to this day. Boatbuilding at Brimscombe ceased in the thirties when the canal became impassable.

49. *Right:* Horse brake with seating for about twenty people on the Stroud-Woodchester-Nailsworth run. I have been unable to discover any details about this photograph, except that the young passenger is probably one of the Peacey family, and I think it is taken outside Dirleton House in Cainscross Road. (A hitching ring is fixed to the wall at this point still). A firm called Arnold operated from Nailsworth to Stroud at one time until they were taken over by the National Omnibus and Transport Company (later called the Western National) in 1920.

W. COWARD
TAILOR &
OUTFITTER.
DYERS
PARK
ALFRED ALDRIDGE.
HARDWARE, BRUSHES &c.

50. *Left:* Roadmending at Town Time before 1914. Before the roads in the area were covered with tarmacadam in the 1930's, they were not very satisfactory, covering pedestrians with fine white dust in summer, and mud in winter. The surface of the main roads was renewed nearly every year but soon there were many potholes and ruts caused by the narrow iron shod wheels of the horse drawn vehicles. The trouble was that the materials used were not waterproof, and once water penetrated the stone and softened it, the surface soon crumbled and disintegrated. The process used in mending the surface was thus: a steam roller would proceed, pulling a piece of equipment called a scarifier which levelled off and loosened up the old surface. Then a thick layer of flint stones was spread over the surface (the heap in the picture had just been deposited there by Mr. White). The steam roller would then crush the stones and gradually after many applications of water, obtained in square tanks from the nearby hydrants, a hard surface would have been pounded.

Here Mr. Webb is having a discussion with Mr. Pegler, while Mr. Whitaker looks on.

51. *Top right:* 10th August, 1910. Crowds turned out in Middle Street to mark the passing of Capt. Jesse Tanner for 25 years the Captain of the Stroud Urban District Fire Brigade, who had died on 5th August aged sixty. There was a lot of friendly rivalry between the two fire brigades as to which would arrive at an outbreak first, but once that question was solved, if both had to stay there the co-operation was outstanding.

52. *Bottom right:* View of Holy Trinity Church taken about 1870 from the site of the new Bisley Road, with Rodborough fields in the distance. The church was built in 1838 as a chapel of ease to the parish church, and became the parish church of the new ecclesiastical district of Holy Trinity, in 1879, as a result of the extensive development which took place at that time. The interior was embellished and reseated in 1882.

The foundation stone of Stroud General Hospital which now occupies the site next to the church was laid in 1874, and villas were built on these gardens from 1882 onwards.

53. Dark Mill in 1906, showing the extent of the mill pond, and the way in which the stone built mills, the railway, the road (and the river and canal) fill up the narrow Frome valley.

This mill had at various times been used as a shear-grinder's mill, cloth mill, dye-house, saw mill, and a manufactory of umbrella sticks, until in 1903 it was bought by Critchley Bros. pin manufacturers. They then used the premises for making wood and bone knitting needles, crochet hooks, and pen holder sticks. This part of the business flourished until the invention of a plastic material called Erinoid, produced at Lightpill, caused it to decline, and Dark Mill was demolished in 1964 to make way for modern buildings for making different products on the same site.

54. Lodgemore Mill. The old mill building was destroyed completely by fire on 14th September, 1871. It was a fine old building, the main part being six storeys high. James Ferrabee, of the local family firm which made the first lawn mower, was commissioned to build the new mill in blue, red and white bricks.

After the fire. The top plate shows the ruins, while the one beneath reveals the scene after the debris had been cleared in February 1872. Houses in Bath Road in the background.

55. *Four plates:* Hampton cars were made at Dudbridge between 1920 and 1932 by the Hampton Car Engineering Co. At first only cars in the luxury class were produced . . . about four a week, but later when cheaper models were introduced about twenty a week were turned out by approximately 100 employees. The chief salesman was the son of Dan Leno. The firm had to close in the end, mainly because it was unwilling to change from craftsman's work to mass production.

Top far left: The offices and part of the works.

Bottom far left: Line of cars inside the test shop.

Top left: Mr. Frederick Smith, the founder of Wicliffe Motor Co. Ltd. having a trial run up the Nailsworth Ladder (gradient 1 in 2½). His firm held an agency for Hampton cars. A 10hp. light car would cost in the region of £375 complete. (Reproduced by kind permission of Wicliffe Motor Co. Ltd.)

Bottom left: 4th September, 1921. The magazine 'Light Car and Cyclecar' organised trials at the Nailsworth ladder, watched by 4,000 people. This Hampton, with fourteen aboard, managed to reach the top.

56. *Top left:* The Midland Railway opened their branch from Stonehouse to Nailsworth in February 1867. It passed through Dudbridge, and was very convenient for the mills and engineering works there. Kimmins Mill had a track laid straight into an upper storey. In 1886 a branch was taken through to Stroud, branching off at the back of Dudbridge House, as shown here. Though the junction was double track, this was for Dudbridge Station. Both lines became single track almost immediately. The third class fare from Stroud to Gloucester the following year on the Dudbridge Donkey (as it was called) was 1/3d. The line was axed in 1966.

57. *Bottom left:* The much-loved railcar at Downfield Halt, where 'old peg-leg' was crossing keeper for many years. This was one of the first two steam railcars used by the G.W.R. when they introduced their 'Motor-car service' between Chalford and Stonehouse in October 1903. They were withdrawn from service in 1917. The cars ran on the hour from Chalford and the half-hour from Stonehouse, taking twenty three minutes for the journey, which cost 9d. return. On the first day the total takings were £20 from 2,500 passengers. Among the men who served the railcars well over the years was Mr. Harold Gubbins, and he was able to take part in the final run (with auto-train) on 31st October, 1964.

58. *Top left:* Imperial Hotel. The occasion and the date are unknown, but judging from the fact that the faces of bystanders have been blacked out by someone, I guess that it is an elite club of vintage car owners, – The Gloucestershire Automobile Club? AD1, the first car registered in Gloucestershire, is third from the right.

Soon after it was built in 1870 the Imperial became the principal hotel in the town under the management of the tenant Mrs Wade, who was assisted by her four daughters. The eldest, Mrs. Lawson, succeeded her mother in 1884. In a brochure of about 1905 full board was advertised for 10/- per day, baths 6d. and 1/- and porridge 6d. There was good or motor accommodation, modern stabling and covered coach houses e. opposite.

Later, special terms were given to visitors to the 'Light car and Cyclecar' annual trials at the Nailsworth Ladder.

59. *Bottom Left:* The Annual Slad Choir Outing is vividly described by Laurie Lee in 'Cider with Rosie'. For one day each year the village became deserted when the inhabitants boarded five charabancs and, catcalling through Stroud, set off down the valley for Weston-Super-Mare.

This may not be the charabanc he travelled in, but it has the same folded tarpaulins at the back, which the choirboys were allowed to sit on and fall off again. Norah, the little girl in the white dress at the back (now Mrs Marriott of Kingscourt) would never have got up to such tricks.

60. *Left:* Bunches of holly adorn the carcasses for the special Christmas display at the largest butchery establishment in Cainscross. The premises were next door to the White Horse Inn and consisted of butcher's shop, slaughterhouse, and cattle pens. The Inn can be seen on the right with the entrance at the front through a porch with a bay window. This has been blocked up recently, but the door scraper can still be seen. The butcher's premises are now part of the Inn, and although one-and-a-half storeys have been added in brick, the angled wall at the left-hand side with the facet below the roof line, makes it identifiable as the same building.

61. *Right:* King Street Parade in the 1920-30's era before various changes took place. On the left behind the tree is Rowcroft House. Originally built as a doctor's house, it became a bank, and was then rebuilt by Lloyd's Bank. Next is the Victoria Rooms, built before the Subscription Rooms, but later turned into shops. Election and other controversial meetings were held on the forecourt, and shopkeepers often found it necessary to board up their windows.

Facing down the street is the Royal George Hotel. For many years the main post-house in the town. It was closed in 1916, then converted to shops, and later pulled down to make way for Burton Chambers. Lewis and Godfrey's is the large shop on the right. At one time they were undertakers as well as drapers.

62. 'An Old Stroud Custom' — A postcard depicting the fishmongers selling their wares from street barrows. The stretch of High Street between Kendrick Street and Swan Lane was their customary pitch, and they were perhaps the last of the street traders to survive in the town.

63. *Top right:* Folly Lane, Stroud. This is one of the many views taken by Mark Merrett (1862–1945) a studio photographer who was apprenticed to Calcott and Tongue. Subsequently he set up his own busines with his brother George at the old Corn Exchange, and then in Russell and George Street. Later he was in partnership with his brother Rayner.

This photograph is typical of Merrett's work, in that he always tried to portray the fact that the Stroud district combines industrialisation and rural simplicity. The cottage has now been demolished and the road widened. It was only a short distance away from the main part of the town.

64. Stroud Choral Society. An open-air concert given on 4th July, 1907 under the baton of their new young conductor Samuel Underwood. They were accompanied by the band of the 2nd Battalion Gloucestershire Regiment on this occasion at Stratford Park. The orangery in the background is still there today, minus its roof and windows.

The Stroud Choral Society began officially about 1848 when the Choral class of the Stroud Athenaeum started to give concerts in the Subscription Rooms, but its real beginnings are perhaps ten years earlier, making it one of the first choral societies in the west of England.

'Sammy' Underwood remained the much loved conductor of the Society for fifty one years until his death in 1958. The previous year a Jubilee performance of 'The Dream of Gerontius' had been held in the Parish Church. He will always be remembered by Stroud people for his unique personality and dedicated musicianship.

65. A Guinea bank-note issued by Richard Miller from his Brimscombe Port Bank in 1817. Miller was an enterprising young man who started as an apprentice with the Thames & Severn Canal Company in their offices at Brimscombe, and rose to become a barge-master. He also combined his trade with that of coal-merchant, coach-proprietor and auctioneer. The bank failed in 1822.